Rear Detachment
the
Mission of Marriage
& the
Military

KATHRYN MCDOWELL BAKER

Copyright © 2020 Kathryn McDowell Baker

All rights reserved.

ISBN: 9798620817108

DEDICATION

To the families of service members in every branch of the United States Armed Forces. My journey as a military wife is not unique as many of you have and will experience like challenges. It is my prayer that, through this book, you will be encouraged in your personal encounters and that you will be convinced that your position, as the family of an active duty service member, is as vital to the protection and freedom of our country as is that of your soldier.

To our warriors who actively serve and have served in the United States Armed Forces, I salute you. Your commitment to the protection and freedom of our country is unparalleled in selflessness. It is my prayer that this book will be a blessing to your family members who are left in the rear when you are away. Thank you for your service.

CONTENTS

	Acknowledgments	vi
	Introduction	1
1	The Lens	6
2	Divorce	11
3	The Sanctity of Marriage	17
4	Mind Renewal	24
5	Rear Detachment Defined	30
6	Dual Allegiance	35
7	When the Cat is Away	45
8	Honey, I'm Home	52
9	Retirement/ETS	60
10	Lessons from the Rear	65
	References	70
	About the Author	74

ACKNOWLEDGMENTS

This book would not be complete without acknowledging my husband and soulmate, SFC Allen W. Baker, US Army, (Ret.). Through your patience, provision, protection, perseverance and push, you have given me the support I've needed to complete not only this work, but to accomplish anything my heart desires. Thank you.

To my children, Allen II, and DeVante', I am humbled that God has chosen me to be your mother. The joy that it brings is as unique as the two of you. Covering you both in prayer, as you grow through the challenges that are commonplace in life, I count it a blessing to witness the two of you becoming the mature, and purposeful adults that God has created you to be. Be Godly in all that you say and do. Always remember to "Ride Life Until the Wheels Fall Off!"

To my very first grandson, NyZir, you are the bee's

knees young man! Your kind heart and humor are unmatched. I pray that your joy of learning increases even more, as you grow into the fine young man that God created you to be. I pray that you remain proud yet humbled in showcasing the gift of athleticism that God has granted you for His glory! Continue to rock out those A's in school and dare to be Godly-different.

To my siblings, Carl, Rita, and Angela I love you collectively and individually. Know that there are lessons that I have learned from each of you and I appreciate you all.

To my parents, Bishop Charles O. and First Lady Cora G. McDowell (deceased), because you taught me that I could do and be anything and that my voice mattered, I have undertaken and completed this work.

Momma, for your consistency, loyalty, dedication, and for teaching me to "Start out the way you can hold out," I say a huge thank you!

Daddy, for allowing me to rant and rave as you sat, quietly and attentively, listening and for always reassuring me in your composed, yet convincing voice that, "All is well," thank you! See you both in eternity.

To my current pastors, Bishop Michael A, and Pastor Malinda Blue, pastors of the Door of Hope Christian Church in Marion, SC, I appreciate you! The lives of integrity that you lead speak volumes to those who will take notice. Thank you for delivering consistency in teaching, preaching, and walking in the ways of God.

To Elder Regena McPhail, I praise God for the gift He has given me in your friendship and Kingdom sisterhood. Blessings upon blessings upon you and your family.

To the anointed Woman of God (WOG) Belinda Hill Alford, these pages cannot contain how God has blessed my life through your gift of prophecy. I am thankful for the years of Godly wisdom you have shared with me. Thank you.

To my paternal and maternal aunties and uncles, and cousins, I pray that I do you proud. To my nieces and nephews, I pray that this undertaking will encourage you to tap into your God-given gifts and use them for His glory.

To all of those who inspired me to write this book, convinced that what I will share has the potential to be of benefit to others, thanks for your encouragement. It is my prayer that this book will deliver on the blessing that you believe it to be.

INTRODUCTION

Marriage, within itself, is a journey whose navigation differs from one couple to another and can be most difficult, to say the least. Add to it, the active-duty military component, and the result is a unique journey for which many are unprepared.

Mine is not a position of licensure, nor do I hold a graduate degree (at the time of this writing) in psychology (undergraduate only), nor have I professionally counseled couples. Rather, my perspective is one shared from a position of personal experience. As deserving of respect as the clinical studies, academic attainments, and professional licensures are, they are not in themselves, substitutes for personal experience. In this work, I'll give you a sneak peek of my personal experiences, in hopes that in doing so, your marriage will be blessed with the tools that you can use in your unique relationship to strengthen your family's bond.

This book offers an in-depth view of some of the obstacles that are frequent in military marriages, and it gives advice on how to overcome and triumph over these challenges. *Rear Detachment: The Mission of Marriage & the Military* gives solid advice on how to cope with deployments, become a vital support system to your military spouse, and how to move your family forward upon the soldier's return.

In *Rear Detachment: The Mission of Marriage & the Military*, you will learn the importance of your role in the success of the soldier's mission away from home. Within the pages of this book, are tips that can assist you in planning and preparing for your soldier's time away from the family. I have also curated mechanisms you can follow to shoulder the extra responsibility and help you to relinquish those roles upon the soldier's return.

The information in this book comes to you as advice only. As with every piece of advice, it is yours to either accept or to decline. I make no claims as to the success of your marriage if the advice given is accepted, and the methods provided herein are practiced.

What is presented here are gleanings and insight gained, mostly in hindsight, from my 33-year marriage to an active-duty soldier in the United States Army. My soldier served his nation for 24 years before his retirement. Personal experience has been my greatest teacher and it is from these crucial life lessons that this advice is offered, and personal convictions shared.

As my personal experience has not been one involving abuse, I refrain from offering advice on issues pertaining to abuse in any of its various forms (physical, emotional, or mental). However, if the circumstances in which you find yourself call for immediate action, please contact seasoned experts, who can provide professional advice, or law enforcement, who have been trained and can aid in such delicate matters. If instead, you are seeking to avoid such relationships altogether or seeking to help someone else avoid them, allow me to submit to you another title whose author has both experienced and written about such matters. Found on Amazon, the book is titled: *You don't have to marry the wrong man* (Hayes, 2019).

Whether your marriage is one challenged by active-duty military service or one challenged by the situations and the circumstances that are common to most marriages, it is my prayer that my individual experiences and the methods I have used and continue to use to triumph over marital challenges will proffer you a new way of viewing your role in marriage. What's more? Applying the methods herein recommended has the potential to result in a union unvanquished!

Now let's get to it

1 THE LENS

One distinctive feature peculiar to every human being is the lens. Simply put, the lens is an anatomical structure that makes up the human eye. Yet, beyond our anatomical lens, we all possess a psychological lens that helps to capture and categorize the information received in our brains. Let's call this lens, "our mind's eye."

It is imperative that we understand that as we go through life's experiences, familial relationships, cultural norms, religious practices, and other such avenues, we subconsciously develop an internal (psychological) lens through which we view the world. For example, why is it that you do not steal (if you don't – I really hope that you don't)? Most likely, some would reply that they were taught better by their parents or, that the Bible instructs against it. Our values and our integrity are developed by and through various influences. Through these influences we develop a sense of what is right and what is wrong. Subsequently, our views of the world around us and its activities and situations are filtered through our concept (lens) of rightness and wrongness that has been, throughout our lives, developed. Understanding this, it is most likely that the lens through which you view and categorize the action of stealing, categorizes it as unacceptable or wrong.

This cognitive lens is our measuring tool for understanding and determining the world around us. In the field of Psychology, this lens is described as an individual's 'worldview'. It is through the influence of this lens that our attitudes, actions, and reactions are shaped, and even our decisions made.

Through the function of this innate lens in our psyche which has been developed over the course of our lives and personal experiences, we accept or reject that which we deem appropriate or inappropriate. It is through this lens (or parallel to it) that we measure life's encounters.

You may be asking yourself, "What does this have to do with anything?". Well, just as the integrity of a building depends on the foundation upon which it stands, so also does the integrity, reception, and perception of this work depend upon the lens through which it is interpreted. For this reason, it is fitting to share the worldview from which these thoughts and experiences are apportioned, and counsel given; that of a Kingdom of God worldview. What is that exactly? Thanks for asking.

A Kingdom of God worldview is the view of the world developed through the will of God, provided through the

Word of God as found in the Constitution of the Kingdom, the Bible. As my King, I am committed to submitting God's governance of my life. My views are based on my perspective as a citizen of the Kingdom of Heaven. The Word of God is the tool by which I measure my thoughts, words, deeds, and overall behaviors. As such, it is also the evaluating tool that governs my marriage and how my home attains balance.

By searching, applying and living by the Word of God and by allowing His Word to govern our lives individually, my husband and I are blessed in our marriage, as a unit. Does this mean that our marriage has been, and now is, excluded from the challenges that are experienced in marital unions (stay tuned for our collaboration on this subject coming soon)? By no means! What it does mean is that, although we experience those challenges, we are guided by our constitution (Bible) in remedying those areas of challenge.

I have deemed it important that you are made aware of the use of this lens firstly, for it is through it that this information is shared. There may be those who readily accept this information and the Godly lens through which our marriage is viewed, and this information shared. Yet, there may be those who will not. Whichever the case, as the author of this work, I feel it my duty to inform you of the view from which this book is written. This, I am persuaded, allows you to make an informed decision as to whether the information contained herein is of benefit to you. I pray that you will find it so.

2 DIVORCE

At first glance, it may seem quite unusual to include a chapter about divorce in a book that is created to enhance the marital relationship. I assure you it is pivotal to the message of this book to include this crucial statistical information. Why? Thanks for asking!

No warrior, who plans to be successful against his enemy, takes on an enemy without first studying him. This information helps in strategizing how best to engage the enemy. "If you know the enemy and know yourself, you need not fear the result of a hundred battles. If you know yourself and not the enemy, for every victory gained you will also suffer a defeat. If you know neither the enemy nor yourself, you will succumb in every battle" ("Quotes by Sun Tzu", n.d.).

Viewing divorce as the enemy of marriage, it then becomes necessary to study or, at the least, note the enemy's tactics in wars previously waged and won. Herein, lies the importance of this chapter.

Studying divorce, a team of divorce attorneys researched and reported data compiled across 115 studies, facts, and rates ("Divorce Statistics: Over 115 studies, facts, and rates for 2018", n.d.). Among the myriad of statistical data reported according to factors that might lead to divorce, there are several that are of interest for the purpose of this book.

According to surveys completed in 2018, it was reported that in the United States of America, approximately 50% of all marriages end in either separation or divorce ("Divorce

Statistics: Over 115 Studies...", n.d.). What this signified is that separation or divorce was inevitable for half (50%) of marital unions in the United States. With such an observation, the odds of getting divorced were equal to the odds of a successful marriage, 50/50.

Undoubtedly, there are those who would accept such a wager as one with pretty good odds, and why not? After all, such a percentage indicates that there is a 50/50 chance that the marriage will last. On the surface, it may seem harmless to enter a marriage armed with the knowledge of the possibility that it may or may not last 'until death us do part'. Yet, what is disturbing and dangerous about developing such an attitude is the mindset that can be a result. The longevity of marriage should not be left up to chance. There's simply no sitting on the fence. The success and longevity of a marriage, barring extenuating circumstances (abuse of any kind, habitual infidelity, etc.), should be based on the commitment to the marriage by those who are vowing themselves and their lives to each other in matrimony.

Let us now look at some additional statistics concerning marriage in the United States. According to the 2018 research reported by the same team of divorce attorneys, the percentage of divorce goes up with each subsequent marriage after the first. It is reported that of 2nd marriages, 60% end in divorce and of 3rd marriages, 73% end in divorce ("Divorce Statistics: Over 115 Studies…", n.d.). With each subsequent marriage, the likelihood of divorce increases.

Statistically, divorce occurs so frequently in the United States that in the average 2 minutes it takes for a couple to exchange wedding vows, there will be 9 divorces ("Divorce Statistics: Over 115 Studies…", n.d.). During the 5-hour wedding reception, 1,385 marriages will end. On average, 1 divorce occurs every 13 seconds, 277/hour, 6,648/day, 46,536/week, and a staggering 2,419,196/year ("Divorce Statistics: Over 115 Studies...", n.d.).

Although these statistics represent a small portion of those provided in the study, they suffice in showing the frequency of divorce in the United States. With studies showing an equal chance of divorcing as there is of staying together and the new trend that shows an accepted view of pre-marital cohabitation (Lascala, 2019), it is not difficult to understand how many have become cavalier in their attitudes concerning the sanctity of marriage.

"The music at a wedding procession always reminds me of the music of soldiers going into battle" ("Heinrich Heine Quotes", n.d.).

As unfortunate a view as this quote may seem, even more unfortunate is the truth of the statistics that lend to its validity.

Now that we have the statistical data that, at the least, points to the formidability of divorce as a foe, let's now look at the strategy for a Godly marriage which, when applied, defeats the foe of divorce.

3 THE SANCTITY OF MARRIAGE

Concerning marriage, the Apostle Paul in Ephesians the 5th chapter wrote: "For this cause shall a man leave his father and mother, and shall be joined unto his wife, and they two shall be one flesh." (Ephesians 5:31, KJV)

Via statistical data included in chapter two, we can deduce the popular opinion concerning the sanctity of marriage. If the rate of divorce is any indication, not much thought is given to marriage as a sacred union. Many are caught up in the glitz and the glamour of a wedding ceremony with all its thrills and frills without considering, seriously, the vows made before God. On the contrary, when we search the word of God, we understand the gravity of the union and His purpose in marriage. This understanding, and the adoption of this understanding (committing to live by it), is key to renewing our minds concerning challenges in our marital relationships and in our lives in general.

Allow me to share on a more personal note. Prior to truly humbling myself to the entire word of God and removing it from the religious space wherein I had assigned it, determining instead to build a relationship with the Writer of the word I, like numerous others, held to the notion that if my marriage didn't 'work out,' I would simply get a divorce and possibly try again later. As embarrassing as it may be to admit, I must honestly say that, even as a young (not seasoned in the faith) child of God, I did not consider His word concerning the sanctity of marriage. I had accepted Christ as my Savior but had not yet come to understand and accept the all-inclusive application of His word to my life. I had not grown to understand that His word was given to govern the lives of His children in every area. I had not come to realize that there was no place in my life over which His word should not have governed. I had His word (Him) in the proverbial box that we often hear about. Once I grew in the grace and knowledge of God, and began renewing my mind, and moved from a place of religion to a place of relationship, I was amazed at the magnitude of commitment and dedication that a Godly marriage required, that I had not before acknowledged.

Sharing a few of my thoughts with my current pastor, Bishop Michael A. Blue (Door of Hope Christian Church, Marion, SC), concerning the sanctity of marriage and unable to express what I sensed happens in the realm of the spirit when two become one flesh, I became even more intrigued by what he shared. Bishop Blue shared insight concerning the bonding that takes place in the act of marriage by making me aware of a hormone that is released during the act of marriage (consummation) called Oxytocin. To understand more concerning God's purpose in marriage, he encouraged me to complete further study on this hormone. At his suggestion, I researched and discovered that it is the same hormone that is released during mother-infant bonding, when a mother breast feeds her newborn. This hormone possesses powerful bonding properties. When released, it affects both the physiological and psychological aspects of an individual (MacGill, 2017). By influencing the physical and mental aspects of a person, Oxytocin has a direct link with an individual's behavior, both socially and emotionally (MacGill, 2017).

In studying the effects of the act of marriage on the brain, author Anna Hodgekiss (2011) interviewed Dr. Arun Ghosh, a General Practitioner who specializes in sexual health. In that interview, Dr. Ghosh revealed that, although this hormone is present in both men and women, the amount of Oxytocin produced by women is higher than that produced by men (Hodgekiss, 2011). Dr. Ghosh shared that, as *the key to bonding*, the release of Oxytocin increases the level of empathy, and he suggests that this increased level of empathy brought on by the release of Oxytocin is, most likely, the reason why women, after engaging in the act of marriage with a man, fall more deeply in love than do their male counterparts (Hodgekiss, 2011). Dr. Ghosh further reiterated the importance of understanding the effects on the brain when a person engages in the act of marriage. This information can be used to help us in understanding God's purpose concerning the sanctity marriage. Dr. Ghosh shared that Oxytocin does not discriminate when released during the union, regardless of whether the individuals who engage in the act are espoused (to each other) or not (Hodgekiss,

2011).

To this same end, Bishop Blue shared that the bonding that takes place as the result of the act of marriage was intended by God to be a lifetime bond. As a result of the fall of man (sin), those who have engaged in the act of marriage with numerous individuals have bonded themselves to each individual and have, as a result, simultaneous pulls (bonds) on their lives. As a true man of God, Bishop Blue does not leave us without the answer, He shared that the only way to break that bond is to go before our Father, repent and ask Him to deliver us from the ungodly bonds we have made.

Here, although only a small example but worth mentioning still, we realize that although the two are often presented as polar opposites, when viewed through the lens of the Kingdom, medical science actually proves the purpose of our Creator, God.

Armed with this bit of information, I pray that you are led to renew your mind as it concerns the sanctity of marriage and that you will commit to applying this knowledge to your life and allow it to govern your decision making moving forward.

4 MIND-RENEWAL

In previous chapters you have been presented with statistical information about divorce; peeked at the sanctity of marriage the way God designed it; and learned what happens in the brain during the act of marriage (consummation). It is necessary to view the topics collectively to get a comprehensive look at their relativity to marriage. There is a view of marriage that the world has, God's divine purpose for marriage, and a scientific study of marriage that validates that purpose.

The frequency of divorce can be viewed as an indication of fallen man and his worldly ideas and methods on how to deal with issues that arise in marriage. Yet, God's design for marriage is that we not put off each other for just any offense, as was the question posed to Jesus by the Pharisees in the gospel of Matthew chapter 19. "The Pharisees also came unto Him, tempting Him, and saying unto Him, Is it lawful for a man to put away his wife for every cause?" (Matthew 19:3, KJV). Jesus responded to them, "4)...Have ye not read, that he which made them at the beginning made them male and female, 5) And said, For this cause shall a man leave father and mother, and shall cleave to his wife: and they twain shall be one flesh? 9) And I say unto you, whosoever shall put away his wife, except it be for fornication, and shall marry another, committeth adultery: and whoso marrieth her which is put away doth commit adultery." (Matthew 19: 4-5, 9, KJV)

Then there is the scientific view that somewhat establishes the divinely ordained purpose of marriage by God, in that it proves that the act of consummation has a bonding effect on the brain. Who knew? God knew! Even without a scientific explanation, it behooves us to obey our Creator through applying the constitution of His Word to our lives in every area, without entertaining the world's way as an option.

As Christians and Kingdom citizens who reside in the earth realm that was contaminated by sin, our marriages are faced with challenges just as they who are not of the Kingdom. Yet, our response to those challenges is not to be the same as the response of those who have not appropriated God's grace in Christ Jesus in accepting His finished work of restoration to a life of dominion. For those of us who are in Christ, we are to walk (live), in all aspects, as the Apostle Paul wrote to the saints at Ephesus in Ephesians the 4th chapter.

"17) So this I say, and solemnly testify in [the name of] the Lord [as in His presence], that you must no longer live as the heathen (the Gentiles) do in their perverseness [in the folly, vanity, and emptiness of their souls and the futility] of their minds. 18) Their moral understanding is darkened, and their reasoning is beclouded. [They are] alienated (estranged, self-banished) from the life of God [with no share in it; this is] because of the ignorance (the want of knowledge and perception, the willful blindness) that is deep-seated in them, due to their hardness of heart [to the insensitiveness of their moral nature]. 19) In their spiritual apathy they have become callous and past feeling and reckless and have abandoned themselves [a prey] to unbridled sensuality, eager and greedy to indulge in every form of impurity [that their depraved desires may suggest and demand] 20) But you did not so learn Christ! 21) Assuming that you have really heard Him and been taught by Him, as [all] Truth is in Jesus [embodied and personified in Him], 22) Strip yourselves of your former nature [put off and discard your old unrenewed-self] which characterized your previous manner of life and becomes corrupt through lusts and desires that spring from delusion; 23) And be constantly renewed in the spirit of your mind [having a fresh mental and spiritual attitude], 24) And put on the new nature (the regenerate self) created in God's image, [Godlike] in true righteousness and holiness." (Ephesians 4:17-24, AMP)

In our marriages, as in our lives in general, we are to measure our responses, our actions, and reactions by the word of God (the constitution for Kingdom of Heaven citizens), as our minds are renewed in Christ, rather than from our old, unregenerate mindsets. The principles we are to practice from the word of God in solutions to our problems, oftentimes, go against the world's (fleshy) idea of solutions to the same. Yet, we are no longer governed by the "old man" in this newness of life that is in Christ, but we are governed by God and are accountable to Him in all that we do and say. We do not escape this accountability even in our marriages.

Now let us proceed from this place and advance further.

5 REAR DETACHMENT DEFINED

The placement of this chapter, which defines the term, *rear detachment*, may appear strange having been included at this point in the book. Yet, it was with forethought that it be included at this juncture. For in the previous chapters, the foundation for the remaining thoughts was laid. It is now, upon those thoughts, that the following conclusions are shared.

Rear detachment, in the occupational dialect of the United States Army, is used to describe the status of soldiers who do not deploy with their units on a mission. This 'detachment' is not merely a physical separation *from*, as one may understandably assume, but simultaneously, it is a separation *for*. Soldiers, who are a part of rear detachment, are separated *from* the physical deployment with their respective units and are separated *for* another aspect of the mission that will be carried out at the home station of duty.

From their position in the rear, and physically separated from their units, these soldiers remain an integral part of the mission as they continue the day-to-day duties at the home station. Their role in the mission, although different in function from the soldiers who deploy, is still purposeful and vital to the overall unit-mission success. Theirs, soldiers in rear detachment status, is a position that may not be lauded or applauded but is, nonetheless, vital to the success of the overall mission of the military.

Overseeing these soldiers and making sure that the overall home-station operations are properly executed, is the Rear Detachment Commander or RDC. The duty of the RDC is to keep the unit functional by manning its various operations and performing the duties necessary in the absence of the deployed Commander. RDCs are appointed by Brigade Commanders and they are provided training and resources in order to help them execute the functions of their added tasks (U.S. Army Rear Detachment Commander's Handbook, 2006).

Like Rear Detachment Commanders who supervise the various operations and perform the duties of the Unit Commander during deployment, it also becomes the task of the spouse of an active duty soldier, to oversee the various components of day-to-day living and to perform duties that aid in the family's success, as a unit, in the absence of the deployed soldier. Also integral to the success of the family during the soldier's intermittent absences (deployments, trainings, or rotations) is the conviction of the spouse that, though separated *from* their soldier, they are separated *for* the family's mission at home. This personal conviction may serve as inspiration for taking pride in and working diligently at the added tasks.

British soldier, military theorist and historian, CPT. B.H. Liddell Hart said: "Man has two supreme loyalties – to country and to family. And with most men the second, being more personal is stronger. So long as their families are safe, they will defend their country, believing that by their sacrifice they are safeguarding their families also. But even the bonds of patriotism, discipline and comradeship are loosened when the family is itself menaced." (Hart, 1954/1991)

Simply put, in order to focus on the mission at hand, whether at home or abroad, a soldier must be convinced that their family is safe and are benefiting somehow from their sacrifice. As the RDC in the equation, it is necessary to handle affairs on the home front to keep your soldier encouraged so that their sacrifice for the country is not to the detriment of their family.

For this to work, it is necessary that the soldier and their spouse be of one mind. "Can two walk together, except they be agreed?" (Amos 3:3, KJV) You must be unified in your commitment and must both understand that your commitment and sacrifice to the mission at home is for the welfare and the stability of your family.

Before we move further, allow me to share a bit about the challenges I faced in coming into agreement with my soldier on this front. It was necessary that I first came to recognize, understand, and accept his dedication and commitment to the military and to our family was one that required a dual allegiance.

6 DUAL ALLEGIANCE

Oath of Enlistment

"I, _____, do solemnly swear (or affirm) that I will support and defend the Constitution of the United States against all enemies, foreign and domestic; that I will bear true faith and allegiance to the same; and that I will obey the orders of the President of the United States and the orders of the officers appointed over me, according to regulations and the Uniform Code of Military Justice. So help me God" (Oath of Enlistment, n.d.)

Traditional Christian Wedding Vows

"I, (Name), take you, (Name), to be my wife/husband, to

have and to hold from this day forward, for better, for worse, for richer, for poorer, in sickness and in health, to love and to cherish, till death us do part, according to God's holy law, in the presence of God I make this vow" (Lorraine, 2017).

The above order was the order in which my soldier (husband) pledged his allegiances. I would soon learn that the order in which he pledged, would be the order in which he determined to honor them. In no way did that mean he was inconsiderate of his family or our needs, but it meant that he had a duty to serve and was determined to honor it and honor it well. He had determined, as a teenager, to be a career soldier and he was on his way to fulfilling that desire. In agreeing to become his wife, it was necessary that I come to grips with the fact that this was the way he had determined to honor his country and provide for his family.

As his family, we would simply come to understand, appreciate and accept his commitment to the service of our country, understanding that it meant he would often be away from the home. In our acceptance of his commitment, we formed a normalcy for our family as it concerned his commitment and dedication to both his country and to our family.

One such norm regarded his leaving for trainings and leaving for deployments. During those times, we would learn the unofficial term associated with the U.S. Army dubbed, "hurry up and wait". This practice ensured that the soldiers be in order and ready to attack the mission at hand at the given hour only to, upon arrival, find themselves in a waiting mode. This "hurry up and wait" practice had the potential to lead families, who had gathered to say goodbye and to see their soldier off on his mission, on an emotional rollercoaster. Families oscillated back and forth between the sorrow in saying goodbye and the joy that the soldier had not yet departed for their assignment away from home. This "hurry up and wait" could last for hours or even days, as times of departure were subject to change without notice or explanation. This could amount to the family saying goodbye several times over a period, which may have been hours or possibly days.

Rather than experience the added challenge of saying "goodbye", "hello" and "goodbye" again, we adopted a practice of saying our goodbyes at home, days before the actual time of departure. On those occasions when I took him to the scheduled departure location, he would insist that I take him, give him a hug (me and the kids), drop him off, and take our children back home to continue with the balance we had struck in our home life. This norm we developed over the years helped me to adapt and adjust more quickly to his absence. Having our children to care for alone was a challenge within itself and we did not want to add to it the emotional rollercoaster of saying goodbye several times. Not having him present to share in their care, it was imperative that I channel my energies into helping them to adapt to his absence which left very little time for pity parties. I needed to lead an exemplary life for our kids. To be their example, it was necessary that I remained composed and showed no signs of distress due to their father's absence, so that our children would more readily adjust into their, "when dad is gone" norm. We could then move forward in his absence, as we awaited his return.

What would be years later, our children would bring to us the realization of the results of our efforts by sharing with us that they had become "used to" (normalcy) their dad's absences. This, in no way, detracted from their dad's role of fatherhood in their lives but their admission, their feedback as adults, helped us to understand that for them, our home life, the way we lived and the way we handled their dad's absences, was their *normal*. We had always been a military family and their dad's frequent departures and arrivals were what they had come to expect as the *norm*.

That which is normal for one family will differ from that which is normal for another. It is necessary to build your family's "normal" based on what works best for you and in your home. Remember, that which those of us who have been blessed to be military families consider normal, may be different from that which those who are blessed to be civilian families consider normal. Normal, in this case, is relative. What is most important is that you build your own normal and remain consistent. Be true to your normal.

Just as the RDC maintains a level of normalcy in the unit that remains attached in the rear by continuing the day-to-day routine of the unit assignments and duties, it is ours to maintain the standard routines in the home in the absence of our service member. This is also imperative for civilian couples whose spouse's job may require them to be away from the family often. Whichever may be your case, develop a norm for your family.

To accomplish this for our family, we continued our family routines, even in my husband's absence. Friday nights were always dubbed "Family Night" in our home. So, it was imperative that Family Night continued, despite his absence. Tacos for dinner, choosing several movies for the night's entertainment, and eating snacks, to include fresh baked cookies (which I would ruin because my husband baked them best) was our family's Friday night normal. Beyond our special Friday nights, all else continued as best it possibly could in his absence. Bedtimes remained the same, rules remained the same, chores remained the same, behavioral expectations remained the same. We carried on, in his absence, as though he was still physically in the home. Not only did this help our children remain at a level of normalcy, it was also of benefit to my husband upon his return.

Allow me to add just a note here. Assuring that children obey both parents is integral to the foundation of the family. Regardless if the family is a military family or a civilian family, it is necessary that children understand that, as parents, we are united in our care and decision-making concerning them. This is important so children will understand that obedience, to adult supervision, is not an option. Today, it is necessary that I defend that previous statement by adding to it that, I am here speaking of responsible, reliable adults as it pertains to adults that our children should obey.

Having added that, it is necessary that children do not deem one parent more honorable than the other. They must understand that together, the parents are a unit and that they must be obeyed equally. It is a sad commentary when adult parents, (I say 'adult' here because all parents are not yet adults themselves), admit that they are unable to handle their children in the absence of the other parent. Unless a child has a developmental disorder (physical, or psychological), this should not be the case. Children should not be trained (and whether it is intentional or by default, they are being trained) that obeying one parent is critical while obeying the other is optional.

Therefore, in our home, we remained united in the view of our children in matters concerning them, even if we disagreed privately. As we understood that our children, in their childlike wisdom, would discern the division and would attempt to use it to their advantage, as most any child would. We could not effectively raise our children, in a home in which their father's career choice meant that he would be away for weeks, months, or even years, if our children were trained that they only had to obey their father yet, I was the one who would remain detached in the rear to continue their rearing. There would have been a real breakdown in the family unit in his absences had this been the case.

I've shared information about the children and keeping the home. Now, let's move a bit further and discuss keeping ourselves.

7 WHEN THE CAT IS AWAY

Thus far, I've shared how we managed my husband's absences due to his active-duty soldier status in the US Army, and how we managed to raise our children in times of his absence. Now, let's talk a bit about how I managed *myself* in his absences.

The multilingual proverb, "When the cat's away, the mice will play" has been spoken for centuries. In its essence, it means that when someone in a position of leadership, headship, or management is absent, those who are subject to that individual's position may use their absence as an opportunity to behave in a way that they would not, otherwise, behave if that individual were present. Truly, we understand that our spouses are not in positions of leadership, headship, and authority *over* us but rather, in partnership, *with* us. Yet, the proverb remains the same, as with their absence comes the opportunity to 'play' as would mice in the absence of the cat. Dependent upon the game(s) played, just as the survival of the mice could be at stake, so also could the survival of your marriage and your family.

Concerning the use of the word 'games' in this instance, I'm referring to those activities in which we participate in the absence of our spouse. What I discovered, during times of my husband's absence, was that there was always an invitation to a function here or an activity there that was not appropriate for a married woman, whose husband was away, to attend. The inappropriateness did not entirely mean that the events were immoral (and yes, those opportunities presented themselves as well) but that my attendance at that function or my participation in that activity in the absence of my husband, could be misconstrued. I know that some reading this may believe that they do not care what others think and, indeed they may not, but when we renew our minds concerning our Kingdom citizenship (remembering the lens through which this information is provided), it is necessary that we apply the portion of the constitution of the Kingdom (Bible) which states, that we "Abstain from all appearance of evil". (1 Thessalonians 5:22, KJV)

Remember (dependent wife or dependent husband), there are female active-duty soldiers as well as male active-duty soldiers. Just as the male active-duty soldiers have civilian wives, the female active-duty soldiers may have civilian husbands and even with the best of intentions, it is not a good practice to habitually spend time with spouses of the opposite sex in the absence of your spouse. Even on the premise of passing the time away or being of support to each other in the absence of your soldier. Comingling too often with spouses of the opposite sex can lead to ideation, accusation, and eventually, confrontation upon the soldier's return.

Such are the stories I've been made privy to. Many are the stories I've heard from soldiers who, upon returning from training, deployment, or rotation, found their spouse in intimate relationships with the soldier's 'friend' or simply a mutual 'friend' who continued to remain close to the soldier's family in his or her absence. In many of the stories, the spouse was very sorrowful and regretfully expressed that they never intended for things to go as far as they had. Yet, because of their desire to mingle, and their failure in showing wisdom, the result is a broken marriage and a broken friendship. In most cases, the person with whom they engaged in an extramarital affair has returned to whatever life they had prior to the affair or, at the least, must deal with the fallout surrounding the situation in their own life.

It is wise to surround yourself with like-minded women (or men) who have the same values about marriage and with whom you can share your thoughts and feelings concerning the soldier's (or civilian spouse) absence. Oftentimes, you will find that others may have information about events and occurrences that you were not necessarily aware of or simply may not have planned to attend. As in any situation we experience, support and direction from someone who has gone through, who are currently going through, or who, in some fashion, has been touched by a like circumstance, can be of great consultation.

In choosing to associate with those who can be of benefit to you and your family as you go through times of separation *from* and separation *for*, be mindful not terminate or devalue the support of others who may have no connection with the military or who may not be able to exactly identify with your current situation concerning carrying on in your spouse's absence for, they too may play a vital role in assisting you through those most difficult assignments. Simply be decisive and intentional about whose support you seek in what area. For example, someone who has never personally experienced the military as a soldier or the spouse of a soldier, is unable to offer advice from a position of experience. Yet, there remain a plethora of other areas in which their advice and opinion is warranted and can be of great benefit. In those areas, listen and take heed.

Whether associated militarily with your experience or a loving, caring friend or family member, there are those who are of great support to you and your family during times of separation from your spouse.

"Listen to counsel, receive instruction, and accept correction, That you may be wise in the time to come." (Proverbs 19:20, AMP)

8 HONEY, I'M HOME

After making great efforts to dig in your heels and make giant strides in balancing the weight of the family in your soldier's absence, what you anticipate most happens- they return!

After the bells have been rang, the whistles blown, and the band has played, every soldier will march into the warm embrace of their eagerly waiting families. Your soldier may be a few pounds lighter and even a year older but prayerfully, no worse for the wear, your soldier returns home.

I remember those occasions and the days leading up to my husband's returns home. As he was, and remains, a very private person, I had to learn to tailor his homecomings to his liking rather than what I deemed appropriate for celebration. Coming from a family who was more emotionally demonstrative, I was always ready to organize a grand affair to celebrate his homecomings yet, it was necessary that I respect his idea of a celebration for, after all, it was for *him*. This usually meant that the celebration would consist of our immediate family. This became our tradition and our norm for his homecomings. His idea of celebration called for me to spend time in the kitchen cooking his favorite meal, baking his favorite dessert, and making whatever special arrangements for things that would make his return home comfortable.

Although his military commitment required that he remain out of the country for months or possibly a year, and we were exuberated upon his returns, homecomings were not always the cut and dry occasion one might expect. There was more to be reckoned with that extended, sometimes for weeks, months, or even years, beyond that initial joy over his return. Adjustments physically, mentally, and emotionally were necessary upon his return. Physically, he had to reacclimate to the time difference and the difference in temperatures. Having served twice during the war in Iraq, his body had to acclimated to temperatures that were unheard of in the United States and would have to reacclimate, over time, upon his return. He had adopted ways to manage the scorching desert temperatures that, when practiced in the states, seemed a bit strange. For example, wearing long sleeved shirts during the hot summer months, after his initial return.

Reacclimating to the time zone was another challenge which could take a physical toll on him both mentally and physically. While in Iraq, depending on which time zone I was in, in the United States, the difference in his time and mine could be 7 or more hours either in the a.m. or the p.m. If the children and I were in Texas, the time difference was 8 hours and if we were in NC the difference was 7 hours. Either way, my mornings were his evenings and vice versa. Imagine the let down when I had prepared so diligently for his return and depending on the hour he arrived, he could barely stay awake and when I was asleep, he was awake.

Returning from a war zone added even greater challenges to the homecoming process. Returning from the war in Iraq, my husband had to readjust to the process of driving outside of a war zone. Although he had not forgotten the mechanics of the driving process, he had become an extremely cautious (slow) driver due to the year or more spent in the war zone. Things that I viewed as trash on the road (paper bags, plastic cups, plastic bags, etc.) he viewed as a possible life-threatening device and would swerve to avoid it. Imagine excitedly giving the reigns of driving over to your spouse, as you have driven for an entire year and simply want to enjoy riding, when suddenly, the car swerves to avoid running over a paper object in the road!

Emotional acclimation is ongoing. The immediate acclimation emotionally to his wife, his children, and his home was sometimes challenged by what he endured while away. Although physically present, he was not always emotionally present and would, at times, become distant. Still now, years later, he still experiences those distant moments. Sometimes they are short lived, and others may take a few days but, I've grown used to it now and no longer try to fix it. I simply allow him to do what he needs to do in order to return to the moment, whenever he is ready. The experience of being blown from a vehicle by an Improvised Explosive Device (IED); losing soldiers in battle; and experiencing the drama that is war (the National Geographic's miniseries, *The Long Road Home,* and the book by Chief Global Affairs Correspondent for ABC News, Martha Raddatz (2007) titled, *The Long Road Home: A Story of War and Family,* chronicles a surprise attack suffered by his Division, First Calvary, while in Sadr City during his time in war in 2004), was a lot for him to process and understandably so.

So, although he was home physically, he was not completely back. Regardless of how anxious I was to relinquish his duties to him upon his return, it wasn't always feasible to simply drop everything in his lap at once with the expectation that he would simply pick up where he left off. He needed time to adjust to life in the states and to life at home again. Not only did he have to readjust to being home, but he was also challenged to readjust to his military duties back in the states after the war. Can you imagine returning to the unit that you left stateside, but returning without many of the soldiers who boarded the plane with you bound for Iraq a year ago? Neither could I.

It takes prayer and wisdom to be a positive support to a soldier upon his return from war. As challenging as my experience was, it paled in comparison to the challenges that many other families endured and continue to endure. By the grace of God, my husband returned home, there were many whose husbands, wives, sons, and daughters did not. Knowing this, we were then and remain, thankful for the blessing, knowing and trusting God to continue to give us strength.

Regardless of whether your service member's deployment is to a war zone or simply a rotation out of the country on another assignment (unaccompanied), use wisdom upon their return. Be prepared to possibly shoulder the extra duties for a while longer, before relinquishing them to the soldier upon their return home. The best plan is to discuss the return before the departure. It's okay and, in my opinion, wise to discuss the expectations that you may have of each other upon the service member's return home to avoid added challenges as the family settles back into a routine that includes the service member.

Remember, although I make suggestions here and share with you from my personal experience, I am sharing what worked for my household and things that were developed as our norms. Yours may differ, and that's fine. Simply be proactive and intentional as you walk through your family's norm.

And just when we had mastered (as much as it can be mastered) the norm, it changed!

9 RETIREMENT/ETS

When, "Honey, I'm home!" becomes "Honey, I'm home to stay!" Here comes an opportunity to build a new norm!

Twenty years have seemingly, flown by and we find ourselves at another crossroad, retirement! What seemed an eternity away, is suddenly upon us.

Rising at zero-dark-thirty for 20 (+) years for physical training (PT), showering and returning to work by 9 am, and working until 5 pm, or whenever they are released, is a career service member's way of life. Add to that, PCS moves, training, and deployments and you have a recipe for what it takes to 'Be All That You Can Be', which was the Army's recruiting slogan during the time my husband enlisted in

1984. Having been all that he could in the military, it was now time to experience life as a civilian.

The culmination of years of military service is an occasion that is filled with mixed emotions. Sure, the service member is elated that they have made such a great and prideful accomplishment but, along with that can come the fear of the unknown for both the service member and their family.

Along with the obvious adjustment from military to civilian life, there is, again, an adjustment in family life. It is this adjustment that can prove to be most challenging for all involved.

With a total enlistment on active duty of approx. 24 years, in his career, my husband's military experience had run the gamut. From PCS moves within the Continental United States (CONUS) to PCS moves outside of the Continental United States (OCONUS), from Fort Campbell,

Kentucky to Mannheim, Germany. From hardship tours in Korea to 2 tours of duty, during wartime in Iraq; he had experienced life as a career soldier to the fullest. After such an extensive career, surely, he was excited and welcomed life beyond the military, as well he should have.

As the wife of a career soldier (married 22 years of his 24-year career), I, too, had experienced life in the military. As a married couple, all we knew was life as a military family. Now, all of that would change and we were somewhat excited and prepared for life after the military, or so we thought.

With all that we had factored in the equation, neither of us considered what it would be like to be together continually. I'm sure that sounds strange but it's true. Our norm had been built around his intermittent periods of absence from the home. Upon retirement, although he eventually found other gainful employment, his constant presence in the home took some getting used to, to put it mildly.

Just as we had not factored in being together constantly, we did not factor in eventually being alone in the home. Of course, we knew and understood that our children would mature and leave home, but it seemed to have blindsided us, especially when our youngest graduated high school and went off to college. Our children had been my focus for all their lives and, suddenly, it was just the two of us. There were times that I longed for our children to be back in the home while he, on the other hand, laughed and continually reminded me that it was just the two of us now; laughing like the evil genius in a childhood movie.

Just as we had built a norm during the years of his active duty service, we would now build a new norm in his retirement. We are now enjoying the experiences of this new norm and are looking forward, with great anticipation, to our next chapter.

Your experience may be that the service member has reached his Expiration Term of Service (ETS) and has decided not to re-enlist. Whatever the situation, when a service member makes the decision to move beyond their tenure in the United States Armed Forces, there is a period of adjustment that occurs. Be proactive and supportive in this transition by arming yourself with all available information concerning the decision. Attend briefings (if allowed), ask questions, and explore the next chapter of life beyond the military.

10 LESSONS FROM THE REAR

Whether a service member physically deploys to a combat zone or remains in the rear, he is still an integral part of the mission. His position is to step up in the absence of those who have physically deployed and maintain the home station of duty in a manner that is beneficial in the absence of and in the return of the unit.

From the position in the rear, the service member may experience added duties or be expected to operate in positions that they would not otherwise be required to operate. Yet, to support the mission at hand, for the benefit of the Army, and to honor their allegiance, they operate in whatever capacity necessary to support the mission.

In 2001, moving away from its slogan of the past 20 years, "Be all you can", the Army introduced a new slogan, however short-lived, "An Army of One" (Associated Press, 2001). The idea behind the slogan was to entice possible recruits, of a new generation, by encouraging them of the benefits of joining the Army (Associated Press, 2001). The slogan, according to U.S. Army Secretary, Louis Caldera's account, was to achieve this by offering the idea that who they would become, after enlisting, would be better than who they were currently (Associated Press, 2001). The now-defunct slogan fostered the idea that the possible recruit was to view themselves as "own force" (Associated Press, 2001). In my opinion, the new slogan failed to capture the overall message of the military which is that of moving *together* in unison. I believe that the slogan had the capacity to relay an entirely different yet, more accurate, truth.

Imagine with me for a moment, the soldiers when they move in unison in formation during a ceremony. Not only are they so uniformly dressed that it is difficult to determine their individual identities apart from the group, but they move together with such precision and in such unanimity that the movement of the many appears to be the movement of one. To achieve this, no one soldier can march to the lyrics of his own cadence. It takes total concurrence to be so identified with the others around them that they are, preferably, identified with them than apart from them. This is, to me, 'An Army of One'.

If you have ever attended a military ceremony, possibly the new recruits graduating from basic training, you may have noticed the challenge in identifying 'your' soldier as they marched by or simply stood at attention among the others in formation. On such occasions, the soldiers are not readily identifiable by their uniqueness or individuality such as their clothing style, their walk or not even how they wear their hair. It is not until they step out of formation, that they can be identified for their distinctive characteristics.

I relay to you; spouse of the service member, that this is the same position that we, those who are or have been left in the rear, separated *from* our spouses but separated *for* the overall benefit of the family and even our nation, should take. We must be willing to walk in concurrence with our military spouse so that we present as one. This position is not one that is easily adaptable to every mindset as it requires a great deal of selflessness and altruism. In this position, one must be confident in their individuality to the degree that they are willing to blend it with that of their spouse to create a formidable union and to do so without feeling deprived of that peculiarity that makes them who they are.

Together, service member and family work sacrificially to provide protection and freedom for our country at home and abroad. Regardless of the mission abroad, the mission at home is of utmost importance to the enlisted member. Let's work together in keeping our nation safe, whether as a part of the mission in the field or a part of rear detachment.

REFERENCES

Associated Press, (2011). U.S. Army unfurls new slogan: "An Army of One". *Desert News*. Retrieved from https://www.deseret.com/2001/1/10/19562756/u-s-army-unfurls-new-slogan-an-army-of-one

"Divorce statistics: Over 115 studies, facts and rates for 2018". Retrieved from https://www.wf-lawyers.com/divorce-statistics-and-facts/

Hart, L. (1991). *The classic book on military strategy.* (2nd ed.). New York, NY: Henry Hold & Company, Inc. (Original work published in 1954).

Hayes, Y. (2019). *You don't have to marry the wrong man.* Lumberton, NC: Hester Wardlaw Publishing

Company, LLC.

"Heinrich Heine Quotes". (n.d.). Retrieved from

https://quotes.yourdictionary.com/author/heinrich-heine/61477

Hodgekiss, A. (2011). Sex: Why it makes women fall in love – but just makes men want more. *Daily Mail* Retrieved from

https://www.dailymail.co.uk/health/article-2031498/Sex-Why-makes-women-fall-love--just-makes-men-want-MORE.html

Lascala, M. (2019). The U.S. divorce rate is going down, and we have millennials to thank: But it's not all roses and diamonds are forever. There's a downside. *Good Housekeeping* Retrieved from

https://www.goodhousekeeping.com/life/relationships/a26551655/us-divorce-rate/

Lorraine, M. (2017). *Inspiration for your Christian wedding* vows. Retrieved from https://www.weddingwire.co.uk/wedding-tips/inspiration-for-your-christian-wedding-vows--c26740

MacGill, M. (2017). Oxytocin: The Love Hormone? *Medical News Today*, MediLexicon International. Retrieved from www.medicalnewstoday.com/articles/275795.php.

Oath of Enlistment, (n.d.). Retrieved from https://www.army.mil/values/oath.html

"Quotes by Sun Tzu" (n.d.). *Goodreads*. Retrieved from https://www.goodreads.com/author/show/1771.Sun_Tzu

Raddatz, M. (2007). *The long road home: A story of war And family*. New York, NY: Berkley

US Army Rear Detachment Commander's Handbook (n.d.) Retrieved from https://www.myarmyonesource.com/cmsresources/Army%20OneSource/Media/PDFs/Family%20Programs%20and%20Services/Family%20Programs/Deployment%20Readiness/Operation%20READY/Rear_Detachment_Commanders_Handbook.pdf

ABOUT THE AUTHOR

Kathryn McDowell Baker was born in Philadelphia, PA and reared in Robeson County, NC by her parents; a non-denominational pastor and first lady. She is the youngest of 4 children with one older brother and two older sisters.

She was licensed in ministry by her father and the True Faith Ministries family in August of 1999 in Florence, South Carolina and duly ordained in the same as an Elder in July of 2012 by the Tri-Unity Christian Fellowship of Ministries, of which her father was founder and overseer. She received her B.S. in Psychology in 2016, graduating Magna Cum Laude from Grand Canyon University.

Kathryn is married to her husband of 33 years, an Army Retired (SFC) with whom she has two children and several grandchildren.

Made in the USA
Monee, IL
06 November 2023

45868688R00052